FIRST BEGIN...

W. E. Crosskill

with illustrations by the author

From quiet homes and first beginning,
Out to the undiscovered ends,
There's nothing worth the wear of winning,
But laughter and the love of friends.

(Hilaire Belloc, *Dedicatory Ode*)

Highgate Publications (Beverley) Ltd
1987

Illustrations

The pictures of Saturday Market Place, Beverley (page iv) and Walkington (page 22) are reproduced by kind permission of Humberside Leisure Services.

The photograph of William Crosskill's portrait (page 2) is reproduced by kind permission of *Farmer's Weekly*.

The picture of Walkergate House, Beverley, (page 3) is reproduced by kind permission from Arnold Jenkinson's watercolor and ink drawing.

Front cover: North Bar, Beverley.

Back cover: Repton.

© W. E. Crosskill, 1987

ISBN 0 948929 08 1

Published by Highgate Publications (Beverley) Ltd.
24 Wylies Road, Beverley, HU17 7AP
Telephone (0482) 866826

Printed and and Typeset in 10 on 11 Plantin by
B.A. Press, 2-4 Newbegin, Lairgate, Beverley, HU18 8EG
Telephone (0482) 882232

British Library Cataloguing in Publication Data

Crosskill, W. E.
    First beginning: a boy's memories of Beverley,
    Windermere and Repton.
    1.   England — Social life and customs — 20th century
    I.   Title
    942.082'092'4   DA566.4

ISBN 0-948929-08-1

Foreword — An explanation

Lord (Michael) Ramsey, the former Archbishop of Canterbury, who shared the author's study at Repton, had generously agreed to write a foreword to this book. 'I remember him so well at Repton,' he wrote. 'I should count it a pleasure and a privilege to write a brief foreword.'

Unfortunately, his eyesight, which was already causing problems, has worsened, and he is now unable to cope with the task of reading the proofs. He has, however, written to say that he greatly appreciates Ted Crosskill's 'setting his Repton story in the context of his times' and he feels that this will 'make it a work both valuable and attractive'.

Preface

There comes a time when one loses touch with childhood and school friends. They, of course, become absorbed in their new and different lives, perhaps in far corners of the earth. Some may die but memories do not, and through them one can recall those first beginnings and enjoy once again those important things in life, laughter and the love of friends.

September, 1987   W. E. Crosskill

Contents

Page

Saturday Market Place, Beverley c.1860. Lithograph by E. H. Buckler.

Those Early Years

'Yorkshire born, Yorkshire bred; strong in the arm and strong in the head.' I shall always maintain that this is the true version of the old saying and that any distortion of it is due to county jealousy — about things like cricket. Anyway, everyone will agree that it is important to be born in a happy place. I certainly was.

I was lucky to be born in Beverley because it is quite the nicest town in the world and that year, 1904, was a very important one for England because some cordial was arranged between France and England and Parliament controlled the sale of alcohol in public places.

Although I wrote that many years ago, my feelings about Beverley have changed as little as the real character of the town itself. It exudes and displays its history in the magnificent Minster, the friendly St. Mary's church and the North Bar which, together with three other gates, guarded the entry to the town in its early days. The spacious Market Place with its formal pillared Market Cross is still the town centre where people chat and shop, though the streets around it are, admittedly, too narrow for today's huge trucks which use and pollute them.

A short walk from the Market Place takes one on to the Westwood, a large area of common land which protects the town from urban sprawl. On one side of it there is a race course and, on the other, an unpretentious golf course, neither of which impedes the walks of families, the games of children or the treks of pony riders.

Although Beverley never had the extreme problems of the crowded industrial cities, that is not to say that poverty was unknown. My great-great grandmother had been extremely poor. Her husband, William Crosskill, who had a small one-man business as a whitesmith, died in 1812, leaving her with seven children to bring up. The eldest, William aged 12, had learned enough about the business through helping his father to enable him and his mother to carry it on — and then expand it. By 1825 he had built an iron foundry and installed what was a novelty in those days, a steam engine to operate some of the machinery. His first major contract was to re-hang the bells of the Minster. This would seem to be a formidable task for a tinsmith but, to him, nothing was too big or too small. He then started to make cast iron lamp posts. Some of them are still in use, bearing his name and lighting up a few of the older streets in Beverley. Some may be found, too, in Hamburg since, some years later, in partnership with Mr. James Malam, he constructed and installed a gas plant in that city.

It was at this time in our history that the system of agriculture in England was, of necessity, changing. The growing population needed more food than was being produced. The farms were being 'enclosed' and converted

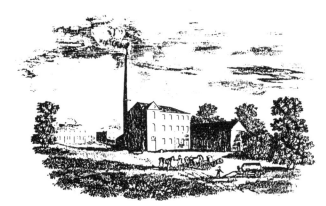

Crosskill Iron Works c.1829.

into viable holdings with larger fields which required heavier implements than the spades and hoes that had sufficed in the past. So William started to make them. Within a few years he was making not only horse drawn ploughs and harrows but carts and wagons of many kinds. His most famous implement, however, was a clod crusher of which, by 1850, he had made some 2,500. These were sold in North and South America, Australia and several European countries. Among other things for export were pre-fabricated four-roomed log cabins for shipment to Australia. Surely this was a case of 'sending coals to Newcastle'!

At that time he was employing 240 men. Through his ingenuity and the industry and co-operation of all who worked with him, the business thrived and expanded still further. By 1853 the small Beverley Iron Works had grown into a factory which covered an area of seven acres off Mill Lane and employed more than 800 men.

His achievement may give the impression that the growing engineering industry in Britain was a bed of roses. In fact it was not. Strikes were prevalent throughout Lancashire and Yorkshire in 1852. William made his attitude towards the unions quite clear in a speech at the Beverley Assembly Rooms: 'Clubs which dictate to your employers are impolitic and always end by injuring the

William Crosskill
(Reproduced by kind permission of Farmer's Weekly).

employed.' He said he would have no hesitation in breaking a strike. 'Had my men in a body done so, I would not have closed my workshop but would have advertised

Crosskill's Clod Crusher, from an engraving in The Farmers' Magazine.

2

Bell's Improved reaping Machine by Crosskill.

for skilful workers in any trade who knew the use of a two-foot rule, compasses and calipers and put them, under good assistants, to my tools, and even worked with my own hands sooner than have closed my workshops.' His employees, then numbering about 500, refused to join the unions and, instead, made a public presentation to him of a magnificent clock as a token of their regard for him as an employer.

In April 1853 he sent his son Edmund to America to show some of his products at an exhibition to be held at the Crystal Palace in New York. The interesting chronicle of the tour he made, covering some 7,000 miles by rail, river and lake steamers, stage coaches, horse buggy, canoe and on foot is a story by itself which will be told later. [See *Appendix*.]

When Edmund arrived back in Beverley in December he found that production at the works was still increasing — and in several different ways. More sophisticated implements such as reaping machines and portable railways for use on farm land were being made and, the next year, when the Crimean War started, the government ordered scores of ambulance-wagons, motors and thousands of shells needed by the army.

This development, of course, required money. Nowadays it would have been provided by floating a limited company but there was then no such thing and the only source of money was from the bank. William had obtained a loan from the East Riding Bank in 1847, secured by a mortgage on the property, but, although the business had flourished and grown since then, the bank foreclosed on it in 1855 at the highest point of its prosperity. The amount owing was about £73,000 and the property was taken over by the bankers as trustees.

At that point William retired and went to live at

Walkergate House.   (*Arnold Jenkinson, June 1967*)

Walkergate House in Walkergate, not far from the Market Place. He was appointed H.M. Distributor of Stamps for the East Riding, a remunerative sinecure bestowed on him as a reward for political services to the Liberal Party. The business was carried on by William's two sons, Alfred and Edmund. But, in 1863, when William succeeded in his claim before the Master of the Rolls that the trustees were abusing the terms of the trust, the two brothers withdrew, bought in their own drawings and patterns from the trustees and set up their own business on a site in Eastgate under the name of William Crosskill and Sons. As for the compensation they received, a sum of £25,000 was mentioned in the Bribery Commission evidence of 1869, an amount equivalent to £¾ million today. (Limited companies were approved by Act of Parliament in 1856. It is strange that the brothers did not use the protection they gave for their new company.)

William died in 1888 and Edmund shortly after that, in 1891, due, it was reported, to having caught a severe cold at the Smithfield Show. Alfred carried on the business until his death in 1904 when it was taken over by the East Yorkshire Cart and Waggon Co. Ltd. Unfortunately I arrived too late to know either my grandfather Edmund or his brother and sister.

72 Lairgate, Beverley.

Home Sweet Home

When I was born in 1904 my father and mother were living at 1 Bar House next to the North Bar but, shortly afterwards, we moved to a house in the narrow old street called Lairgate. It had the most unprepossessing brick frontage imaginable but, inside, I thought it was lovely; it was home. It is still there so I went to see it not long ago. I rang the bell, was ushered in and then I said, 'I haven't been in this house for more than seventy years. We used to live here. May I please look around?' They agreed readily and became interested themselves. They were running a local government office.

The hall looked just the same as I remembered it with black and white tiles on the floor and the staircase leading up to the drawing room, the bedrooms and the 'prison' area, our day and night nurseries. The fireplace and the large picture window in the dining room were the same, too. 'We must keep it like this', they explained, 'because it is a listed house.' The only difference was, of course, that, instead of our furniture and little treasures, there were desks and filing cabinets.

We went upstairs. The drawing room had always been my favourite place. It had the same lovely view across the garden as the dining room below it, and my mother's huge piano with lots of photographs of people on it. My father used to play it sometimes but he had to put sort of rolls into it and then pedal furiously. But the most interesting things to me had been the bits of china, silver, miniatures and things we were told were 'bric-a-brac'. These we were forbidden to touch or move.

We then moved on, through the baize door and into the 'prison' area. I showed them the window through which I used to wave to mother if she came into the garden which meant, 'PLEASE can we come down?' We then went to the back stairs down which we could sometimes escape with the connivance of 'Cookie' and Annie, our cook and housemaid. They were sisters, Esther and Anne Allenby, who were our great allies and helpmates for many years. I remember mother engaging them over the telephone. They were to be paid £1 a week each, plus a dress and uniform. After my mother died in 1912 they relieved our sad distraught father of many of the needs and cares of his three growing children. Some years later Annie married and went to live in Canada and Esther returned to her home in Lincolnshire. We were very sad when they left.

My Domain

Before thanking my escort and leaving the old house in Lairgate, I had seen from the window that the lawn I remembered had become a car park paved with tarmac. When it was a garden I had thought of it as my domain — not one that I ruled over with a rod of iron (if anyone did that it was Mr. Rollinson, the old bearded gardener who must have been well over thirty), but I thought of it as that because it was about as big as I could cover on my tricycle.

After the lawns near the house (not forgetting a super peach tree on the wall below our nursery window) came

beds of roses and other flowers in their seasons. Paths crisscrossed these and led to more lawn and then some big trees, one being a weeping willow. Beyond them was the tennis court, more flower beds and then a paddock. Along the side of this a path led to a door in the wall which opened on to a lane near the Westwood — end of domain! All that was on *one* side of the garden, the other being taken up mainly by a vegetable and fruit garden with a wall all round it. Nearer to Esther's domain, the kitchen area, there was a greenhouse and a potting shed. I used to cart stuff from there for Mr. Rollinson in a trolley I towed behind my tricycle. He could have done this more quickly himself in his wheelbarrow but he was too kind to say so. What a lovely, enjoyable and happy place the garden was but, I suppose, one must not grudge part of it now being a car park: it keeps cars off the streets.

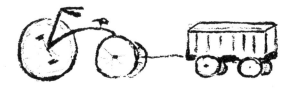

Those Wretched Walks

Gardening was my favourite thing and I soon had a small plot of my own so I was always annoyed when I was summoned to go for a walk. These were all right in a way but, after we had done the same one two or three times, it became boring. Before I was six Nanny and I knew them all backwards. The Market Place was always interesting because there were so many people and shops and things, but we weren't allowed there often and, anyway, it was no good for bowling hoops because of the cobbles. The only walk we never got tired of was to the barracks to see the soldiers drilling in their scarlet tunics. This, however, was rather a long walk and, on the way back, I used to cling to the side of the pram in which my young brother sat warmly and smugly.

Walks on Sundays were the worst because it meant I had to wear my sailor suit. It had a silly blue collar hanging right down my back with white lines on it and, in front, I had a sort of black scarf. My hat was a big floppy straw thing which was hopeless in a wind. The only good thing was the whistle which hung round my neck on a black cord. This really was useful. But after once disgracing myself it was always taken from me before we went to church.

The one up New Walk was not bad. After passing through the North Bar we always stopped to look at the pictures and other interesting things in Mr. Elwell's shop. Then we hurried past Dr. Gregory's door in case he leapt out and removed our tonsils or something. The rows of huge chestnut trees then started. Below them, at times, we used to pick up millions of conkers which we stuffed into the pram and my pockets and took home to harden. We

would scurry past the Court House where my father used to go since he was a J.P. because it was gloomy and ugly and I was always eager to reach the next and far more interesting place, the cemetery. When we got there I used to bombard Nanny with question after question about why, how, when and who.

On the way back we went past my girl friend's house and I always looked anxiously at the windows in the hope of getting a glimpse of her. Perhaps it is an exaggeration to call her my girl friend because I had never spoken to her and she may not even have noticed me in the draper's shop where she was buying something. Nanny was waiting her

11 New Walk, Beverley.

turn to do the same thing but, when I edged nearer to the girl, Nanny pulled me back and whispered, 'She has just had measles. Keep away.' I was miserable for some days, wishing that I could have measles too. Funny things girls can do to one.

Our last stop was always at my grandmother's house. She was my father's mother. She was rather awe inspiring to me and looked very like the pictures I had seen of Queen Victoria. She always wore a black dress with sequins on it and a little lace cap and sat in an arm chair with her feet on a stool and a Yorkshire terrier by her side. However, she always gave us biscuits with pink icing on them and I felt very sorry for her when father told me that her husband had died many years ago.

Some Blessings and a Baptism

What was life like in those days? Not too bad I suppose. Cookie's food was as good as was considered suitable for our age group, then 6 and 3. Annie kept the coal fires burning and Nanny was kind to us, although we thought her rather domineering. As for our parents, no doubt they had occasional differences of opinion and some difficulties to cope with such as Income Tax being raised from sixpence in the pound to a shilling and our getting measles or whooping cough but, on the whole, they led a very happy life. There were tea or dinner parties, bridge or musical evenings, dances and theatres, tennis parties and visits to and from friends and relations. There was never a dull moment for them. Both Father and Mother (there were few Dads and Mums in those days) enjoyed gardening and bicycling but, while he played golf, she preferred tennis and croquet.

Father was a practical man, good at fretwork, Meccano and mending things generally. One day he fixed up an electric wire from the kitchen to the tree under which we had tea on tennis party days. I can only guess what the distance was but it must have been more than the length of a football ground. Father would press a button fixed to the tree and this rang a bell in the kitchen. By using a sort of Morse code arranged with Annie at the other end, he could ask for anything extra to be brought. For instance *dot dash dash* meant more cake wanted and so on. Annie would then hurry over with it, panting but with a smile of triumph and never a grumble.

I can only recall one difference of opinion between my father and mother and that was in St. Mary's church where we had gone to have my baby sister christened. When the vicar took her in his arms and asked, 'What is the name of this child?' my mother replied, 'Dorothy Mary'. 'Not at all,' said my father. 'It is Dorothy Florence.' And so it was. He liked my mother's name, Florence, so much that he intended to perpetuate it.

Travel and Trouble

How did people get around in those days? I was all right on my tricycle and father taught me to ride on the step of his bicycle. Mother had a bicycle too but they couldn't go to a dance on them. Grandfather had had a carriage and horses but now the stable yard was empty. Just before I was born father had a White steam car. As far as I can gather it could carry one passenger seated beside the driver and their seat was on top of the boiler which was heated by a methylated spirit burner. It seems, however, that few people were prepared to risk the boiler bursting and, anyway, it was hardly a suitable vehicle to take my father and mother around at night to the dances and theatres they enjoyed. So, when they went to one of their favourite Gilbert and Sullivan operas in Hull, they would come to say good night to us, Mother looking beautiful in a long evening dress and Father very funny in a tail coat and a white tie, and then drive to Beverley station in a hired horse-drawn cab. They then went by train to Hull where another cab would take them to the theatre. So far, so good, but imagine the return journey late at night in winter!

Robert in the Maudslay.

that faced backwards, I could never see how Robert drove the thing. One morning, therefore, I went down to the garage to find out. Robert was washing, dusting, cleaning and polishing the beautiful machine and in no mood to talk to me. So, annoyed with him for being so surly, I licked my fingers and wiped them on one of the brilliantly shining head lamps. Horrified at this act of desecration, he shouted, 'Do that again and I'll knock yer bloody head off!' I was away, streaking up the drive  before he could carry out this threat and, when I reached the house, I went to the kitchen for safety. The cook, a kindly old lady who often gave me cakes and things, was there, busy as usual. For some reason I have never been able to explain I said to her — quite quietly, 'Do that again and I'll knock yer bloody head off!' The poor woman screamed and went away to report me to my grandmother. I had no more runs in the country for the rest of that visit.

My grandfather was less shocked and, though he supported my grandmother in her disapproval of my unpardonable conduct, he had either forgotten about it by the next day or tacitly forgiven me. They were an admirable and lovable couple. They married when young and raised a family of six children. Life must have been a struggle then because grandfather started his working life as an apprentice and then a junior clerk in a shipping office with no influence and no money. Through a combination of hard work and wisdom he rose to become head of the

The next step up the ladder of locomotion was taken by my uncle who lived in Hull. He bought a motor cycle and sidecar. This was splendid for him and my aunt in fine weather as they were very adventurous, but it would not have suited my mother's parents, Edwin and Anne Fenton, who lived at Sutton. In 1910, they got a proper car, a Maudslay limousine, with a chauffeur called Robert to drive it.

Some time later when I was staying with these grandparents I was taken for some drives in the country in it but, as I always had to sit on one of the little tip-up seats

firm and a rich man. At the same time he had several hobbies and enjoyed life. Above all he was a keen fisherman. On several occasions, when I was about nine, he took me with him when he went to fish his favourite trout stream near Driffield.

I used to watch him interestedly for an hour or so and then sneak off to a nearby farm where the kindly housewife would always give me a good stodgy Yorkshire meal. One day he took me fishing in Bridlington Bay in a rowing boat but, landlubber that I was, I was sick most of the time.

Later he felt an urge to see more of the world and went to New Zealand — for the fishing of course — and another time to Egypt. Wherever it was, he took scores of photographs and, on his return, we would sit spellbound looking at them, made into slides and shown on a screen by his magic lantern. He was a keen billiards player and carpenter, too. Many were the toy swords, shields and knick-knacks that he made for me and others of the family. What a pity that people like those grandparents don't live for ever.

Accidents Will Happen

We may laugh now about my father's steam car, my uncle's motorcycle and side car and my grandfather's old limousine but, 15 years later, I had a more hazardous journey than any they experienced. It was in 1926 when I was working as an apprentice in an engineering works at Auxerre in France. I played football for the town team and, when we had an away match, I used to go on my motorcycle, a Terrot, rather than by train.

One day when we were to play at a small town about thirty miles away I set off as usual but ran on to some sharp broken stone and burst a tyre. Luckily I only had to push my bike about half a mile to a village where a kind man lent me his *bicyclette grand sport* and said he would look after mine. So off I went with my boots slung round my neck and a small bag tied on to the handlebars. But, alas, when I had done a mile or two, one of the pedals came irretrievably adrift and I had to push the thing uphill and free wheel down. At the next village, realising that time was running out, I left the cycle and hired a car. This, however, failed me too. After less than a mile the tie rod of the steering fell on to the ground as I was passing over a railway level crossing. So, with my boots slung round my neck and carrying my little bag, I started to walk. Hitch-hiking was then unheard of and cars were few and far between but it was then that my luck changed. A large car, heavily laden with children and baggage and obviously off on holiday, drew up behind me. When I explained my predicament the man, in the true spirit of the *Entente cordiale*, said, '*Montez vite.* I'll take you to the ground.' I squeezed in and he did. We arrived just as the whistle blew for half time. However, I then had the satisfaction of scoring the only goal of the match. (P.S. Every word of this is true.)

Mother.

Sorrowful Days

Soon after my sister was born in 1910 my mother became ill. She was normally such a healthy and athletic person that, initially, this was not regarded as serious — not even, perhaps, by the doctors. But it turned out that she had diabetes. Insulin was then unknown and the doctors could only prescribe a diet which consisted mainly of featherweight bread rolls and recommended that she should move to the seaside. My father acted promptly and we moved, lock, stock and barrel, to Bridlington where he rented a house while one was being built for us — on the very edge of the cliff where the air came unpolluted straight from over the sea.

During that time a governess came to look after us in place of Nanny. Pip was a jolly and much younger person who joined in all the games of hockey and cricket we played on the sands as well as the sea bathing. We had a tent down on the beach for use as a picnic centre, a shelter from the wind and a changing room. It was in this one day when Pip and I were stripping off our bathing costumes and drying ourselves that I saw for the first time how lovely and fascinating women's bodies can be. She must have noticed my interest because, thereafter, she always wrapped a towel well round herself.

One day, a month or so later, Pip told my brother and me that mother would shortly be leaving us and that we should go up to her room to say good-bye. Perplexed, we went upstairs and saw mother lying in bed smiling at us as usual. After a while we kissed her and left the room. Only some time later did we understand the tragic fact of her death and, later still, realised how father must have suffered alone since we were too young to be of any comfort to him.

It is said that the eyes of new born babies see everything upside down. Thinking of this some years later when I was beset with worries which were mainly imaginary and happily transient, I wrote:

'I think I can remember, Mum, the day when I was born,
When you and everything I saw to me was upside down.
Now time has passed and things have changed, the scene sad and forlorn,
And you, I know, were the right way up and the world was upside down.'

A Flight and a Fright

Life went sadly on and we moved into our new house. I started to go to a day school but found the lessons dull and uninteresting. Suddenly, however, something exciting happened. I flew in an aeroplane. A Mr. Blackburn announced that he would be coming to Bridlington to demonstrate his new monoplane. I didn't hear about this until just before it was due to start. The only newspapers I read in those days were *Comic Cuts* and *Rainbow*, neither of which contained any aeronautical information and the news had not reached me on the under ten grape vine. Cookie told me about it, she knew everything. So I jumped on my bicycle and rushed down to the fair ground. This was a large field in which circuses and agricultural shows were held. As it was mainly downhill I arrived at a pretty high sub-sonic speed and dashed into the crowd. I left my bike against a fence — people didn't steal much in those days — and squirmed and wormed my way through the mass of onlookers until I could see the plane taxi-ing towards a sort of platform. It was a thrilling experience: I had only seen pictures of aeroplanes before and the chutter of the engine and the smell of oil added to the excitement.

When the engine stopped, Mr. Blackburn announced through a sort of loudspeaker that he would take a girl and a boy for a flight. Before he had said another word I was off, fighting and pushing my way towards him and arriving at the same moment as a small girl with pigtails in a white dress. Mr. Blackburn congratulated us on being first and strapped us into the front seat while the crowd cheered. In a moment we were off. The girl smiled rather wanly at me and I should think I did the same to her. Up we went and, in a minute or two, we had a wonderful view of the town, the sea and the crowd below us. It was simply grand. Clearly this was the way to travel in the future. But then it changed. I thought that something had gone wrong with the plane — or Mr. Blackburn. We suddenly roared downward and then swooped up and over in what I learned later was looping the loop. Before we had recovered from that surprise we began to turn over and over sideways. After that I don't remember what it did. I had my eyes shut tightly and was just hanging on grimly. However, it was all right in the end and we swooped and landed. I opened my eyes and saw that the little girl was a peculiar green colour — and I think I was probably the same. I jumped down as soon as possible, ran behind a hut and was violently sick. The mistake we had made was to start running before Mr. Blackburn had finished speaking. I only heard later that he had said that he would take any girl and boy up who volunteered to fly with him while he did an aerobatic display.

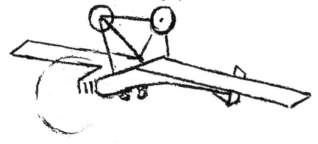

Painful Education

After this thrilling but rather alarming experience school seemed more boring than ever. After a year I had learnt as nearly nothing as possible. The only things one mistress taught me were the county towns of England and the rivers on which they stood. Cornwall intrigued me most because its county town was on the oddly named River Camel. Then, as I was shortly to go to a school

at Windermere, it interested me to know that it was in Westmorland, the county town of which was Appleby. I was a dull, slow, uninterested pupil but, even had I learnt those facts about every one of the counties in the British Isles, I don't think it would have benefited me in later life.

However, the time soon came for me to go to the prep school at Windermere called The Old College. I did not realise until much later what an excellent school it was. When I went there for the first term, Father took me. It meant going to Leeds by train and then on another through Kendal. The rambling school buildings in grey stone were, I suppose, impressive but, at that time, I would have given anything to be back at home. The main entrance was through an archway in a big square tower in which, I felt sure, there would be a dungeon.

The lessons next day gave me a rude shock. It was quite clear that I was, and deservedly, the bottom boy of the bottom class. Nobody was interested in county towns: it had to be Latin, French, arithmetic, history and other, to me, abstruse subjects. I remember well my first lesson in Latin for which Mr. Marcus Raikes, the headmaster's son, was our teacher. He wisely started on something we could all understand, the jingling rhyme that goes:

'*Sum* I am a gentleman, *es* thou art a fool,
Est he is the biggest ass who ever went to school.'
The next step wasn't too difficult either — although Mr. Raikes, for some reason, said it was 'imperfect'. It was something like, '*A ram, a ras, a rat.*' The one he said was 'perfect', however, beat me completely: '*Fui, fuisti, fuit, fuimus, fuistis, fuerunt.*' What nonsense! He made me

The Old College, Windermere.

Quel âge as-tu? Comment t'appelles-tu?' and I soon found I could ask these questions myself. It was a start. I began to develop a memory too. To this very day I can gabble off the names of the first thirty boys on the school roll as they were more than seventy years ago.

Hobbies, Hope and Glory

During the next four years we were taught much more than the three R's. In addition to football and cricket we were taken once a week in the summer term by train to Kendal to swim in the baths. We had a miniature rifle range in the school grounds, a dark room for photography and a carpenter's workshop. We also learnt to sing, make hay and collect caterpillars.

Every Saturday evening the whole school gathered together for a sing song. This always concluded, like the Proms, with *Land of Hope and Glory*, which made the whole building shake. In between songs the music master would play short pieces on the piano or get one of his star pupils to do so. One of them had the amazing ability to give the name of any note the music master played — without looking. It seemed magic to us.

Making hay was a pleasant change. The farmer next to the school grounds was in difficulties because his two sons had gone to the war so Mr. Raikes said we should all go there to help him. We soon got the hang of it and tossed

repeat it word for word but, even after that, I failed to go it alone. He then offered me sixpence if I could recite it. I couldn't. I just sat, tongue tied and with a tear or two in my eyes, ashamed and confused.

Luckily for me, however, the masters and the two mistresses were patient, persevering and encouraging rather than exasperated and angry and my mind started to work. I don't think I learned much French from Mademoiselle Georgette Vautrin but she was lovely to look at, and the cheerful French master, Monsieur Delacourcelle, used to come stamping down the passage to his classroom shouting, *'Bonjour, comment allez-vous?*

and raked the hay, loaded it on to wagons and then stacked it. In return the farmer gave us lots of ginger beer and cakes.

It was Mr. Mallinson who taught us about caterpillars. We used to keep them in tin boxes with air holes punched in the sides, feed them until they turned into chrysalises and then wait for them to become moths and fly away. We really enjoyed his nature study talks and walks. I wrote to my father saying:

> Mr Mallinson is an expert at everything, geography, fotography, pornography and all the things that scientists know about. He can tell us the names of all the flowers and birds and things and how to find crayfish in the streams. Last week he explained to us how the mountains grew and too why it rains so much here.

The Lake District is quite the rainiest part of England but at the school we learnt to ignore this. There was never a case of 'Rain stopped play'. If the football grounds were very wet and soft, we didn't use them — not because we might get our feet wet but because, to do so, would damage the turf. We would then don our football shorts and sweaters and go for a run over the fells.

It was in one of these extra-mural activities that I had my first 'success'. I had gone in for photography with a ten-shilling Box Brownie camera my father bought me and I developed the films and made the prints myself. I was particularly proud of one I had taken of a friend of mine planing a piece of wood in the carpenter's shop and sent it to the Editor of *The Amateur Photographer*. My cup of happiness was full when it appeared in the next issue of their magazine — until I read the caption below it: '*A typical example of over exposure*'.

The Rude Awakening

By the end of the first term I had realised that life was a pretty serious business and, to get anywhere in class or at games, one had to work hard — and strive even harder. For one thing I had seen our soccer team beat another prep school 18 – 1, and I was determined to reach the dizzy heights of the 1st XI myself. I knew also, only too well, that, academically, it was going to be a long haul. To my surprise I was given a book as a prize for 'Conduct' at the end of that Christmas term. It was a calf bound edition of *Charlemagne*. But this only meant, of course, that I was watching the bowling carefully and liked the staff. I was only in awe of one man, the headmaster, Mr. Raikes. While I was in the bottom form I only came into contact with him once a week — for a scripture lesson on Sunday evenings. His bark may have been worse than his bite but it used to put the wind up me and, sure as anything, *some time* during each of those lessons, I had to raise my hand and ask to leave the room. If he mentioned something about Moses striking the rock and the water gushing out

— that did it and up went my hand. It was the same every Sunday but, luckily, he thought I must need medical or surgical attention and this was mentioned in my end-of-term report. Father was worried and called in our doctor who examined me and then said, 'I must circumcise him' — and he did. It made no difference, of course, but, next term, I realised that Mr. Raikes was not so dangerous as he sounded and all was well. A reprimand from him was like the roar of a lion but rarely did he cane anyone.

My recollections of the next year, 1915, are few. It was probably a case of 'All work and no play makes Jack a dull boy.' I certainly must have worked hard because, to my astonishment, I won a prize for 'General Work' at the end of the Easter term. It was another beautifully bound book called *Westward Ho!* Mind you, it didn't signify any very great achievement because it was inscribed 'General Work. Form 1a', only half a step up from my then familiar Form 1.

Wartime

I recall very little abut the war against Germany which had started in August of the previous year. It went on and on but seemed to make very little difference to us in our Lakeland fastness. We did notice, however, that we were called upon to sing the hymn *For those in peril on the sea* more often than usual in church on Sundays and the vicar prayed a lot for our forces overseas. But, as he mumbled these pleas to God almost inaudibly, we didn't learn much from him. Mr. Raikes had put up a large map of France on one of the school notice boards and used to pin little British, French and German flags on it to show where their armies were. But, after the Germans had pushed us back from Mons and we and the French had, in turn, driven them back to the Marne, there was little change in the line from the Channel to the Swiss border along which the entrenched armies faced each other for nearly four years. During that time, as we learnt later, there were periodical attacks and counter attacks in which millions of lives were lost — and national economies ruined — senselessly and needlessly. But, when it ended, we all cheered and waved our flags while the wise resolved that common sense must prevail over national hysteria in any future international dispute. In the meantime all we could do at school to help was to eat less and grow up to become good soldiers in the next war.

In fact we never went hungry. I suppose the meals could be described as plain but adequate. The only real shortage was of meat and, as I had never liked that much — except for the gravy on Yorkshire pudding — I did well, as I could always exchange my portion for a bit of someone else's delicious vegetable pie or a piece of good stodgy pudding. For any whose appetites were still not satisfied, however, there was a further safeguard against famine. The Monitors had what was called a lodge. It was really just a hut in the grounds in which there was a small stove. The hungry used to snare birds of any kind, pluck and roast them and together with some potatoes obtained from the gardener, chipped and fried, they had surreptitious but not very appetising meals.

There were very few luxuries at school, of course —

except when Alice, the matron, invited two or three of us to her room and gave us scrambled eggs with chopped tomatoes. (This is still one of my favourite dishes.)The really luscious things, however, came from other sources. The school could buy no more food than was specified on our ration cards but parents, in one way or another, managed to supplement this and send each boy back at the beginning of term with a tuck box filled with delicious things such as jam, marmalade, cake and biscuits. Cookie used to busy herself making these, Father subscribed his chocolate or sweet ration and I scrounged a few things from the farms on which I worked during the holidays as my 'war effort'. I should add that we didn't have free access to these goodies when we returned to school: they were carefully dealt out by Alice and passed round the table on a communal basis.

Seldom did I run out of pocket money, which may have been ten shillings a term. Occasionally, however, having spent too much on films for my camera or tuck or something, I wrote to Father asking for a little extra. As he knew that I should not be able to cash a postal order and there were at that time no currency notes for less than a fiver, he used to cut a piece of cardboard the size of the envelope, put two or three shillings and sixpenny pieces into slots cut in this and post it to me — with a penny stamp!

Heavenly Holidays

The three terms in the year were a little longer in those days than they are now and there was only one half-term holiday a year. This was two days in midsummer. The prospect of this was tremendously exciting and plans for it were made weeks ahead. Father used to book in at Rigg's Hotel by Windermere station and reserve seats for us in a coach. The sports were held on the Saturday afternoon, a colourful occasion on which most of the fathers wore their most highly coloured striped blazers, white flannels and straw boaters. All the mothers had beautiful long frilly dresses and huge hats, sometimes decorated with imitation flowers or bunches of grapes.

There were two prizes, each a silver cup, for every race. I didn't get one myself. Father just said I must wait until my legs were a bit longer. After a sumptuous tea in a marquee the prizes were given and the winners congratulated. Then Mr. Raikes made a short speech, Mrs. Raikes smiled benevolently at all the parents, and that was that — until the next day and the coach drive. The coach, by the way, was not one of the long ugly tramlike petrol-driven monsters of today but the real thing of the Dick Turpin era, drawn by four horses. Sitting high up in the air beside the coachman one had a perfect view of the

country along the lake shore to Ambleside and, beyond, to Ullswater where we would stop for a picnic lunch.

On one of these half-term holidays, instead of a coach drive, we crossed the lake on the ferry from Bowness and went to a garden where the people grew nothing but strawberries. They said we could pick as many as we could eat — on the spot. We did our best but the result was some trouble with our stomachs and we decided to do the coach drive again next year.

On the return journey, whether by coach or on the

Father and Mother with Grandma Fenton at Goathland, June, 1911.

ferry, the nearer we got to Windermere, the sooner was the parting from parents, who did their best to cheer us up by saying that we should all be home shortly for the summer holidays. That helped because those holidays were sheer joy. Each summer father used to take a cottage for us for the month of August in a little village on the Yorkshire moors called Goathland. Charming though it is, it would drive a town planner mad. It sprawls without rhyme or reason and has, obviously, just grown like Topsy. But long may it remain so.

The railway station is at the bottom of a steep hill. It had to be there in order that the line could be on a sufficiently gentle incline to take the train safely to Whitby. There had once been another line, a much steeper one, on which trains had to be hauled up and lowered down between Goathland and Beck Hole. Mystery surrounds the accident that occurred when the cable snapped and that alignment was abandoned but it now provides a pleasant walk. A stiff climb up from the station takes one past the 'Local' and in view of the two shops. Shortly after that the road divides, one going northward and the other south. Whichever one takes, there are dangers and hazards because the golf course runs along both sides of each. The road pattern is far from being convenient, particularly for the vicar. If, for example, he had come by train from anywhere, after climbing the hill from the station, passing the shops and reaching the 'T' junction, he would have to turn right and walk about half a mile, against flying golf balls, to get to his home, the vicarage. If on the other hand he had wanted to go to his church, he would have had to turn left and walk about a mile to get to it. Higgledy-piggledy it certainly was but, no matter, it was beautiful, friendly and great fun.

About a dozen other families besides ours used to go there regularly each year so we had a very happy holiday community. In addition to the haphazard little golf course, there was a tennis court at the Parish Hall and a cricket ground behind the pub where we used to pit the slight and immature skills we had learnt at school against the slogging of the village blacksmith and other burly locals. On really hot days we would go for a swim, diving from the top of a waterfall into a deep pool of ice cold water in the fast flowing stream at Darnholm. Occasionally we would go by train a few miles down the Whitby line, alight at the next station and spend the day rowing on the Esk. But equally enjoyable were the long walks over the beautiful moors, purple with heather, and along the woodland streams. We ventured further and further each time and, one day, I bet five shillings that I could walk to Castleton and back in a day which, we reckoned, was about thirty miles. Pip came with me and we did it. In some of the later years when, between us, we had two little cars, a bull-nosed Morris and an Austin Seven, we would pile in and drive to Whitby for a Saturday night dinner dance at a rather splendid hotel. It was there that youthful romances grew which had come into bud at the less sophisticated dances at the Parish Hall.

Was there no serpent in this paradise? I only remember one. We never thought of ourselves as tourists — or trippers as they were then called. We were part-time residents. So when motor coaches (then called 'chars-a-bancs') began to bring scores of invading holiday makers

Mallyan Spout.

19

into our territory, we decided to discourage them. The main attraction was the Mallyan Spout, a small but picturesque waterfall about half a mile walk from the hotel. One moonlit night about a dozen of us, armed with spades, picks and shovels, dug an alternative course for the stream which supplied the water for the fall. The diversion was successful and, for a few days, there was consternation in tourist circles. We were wrong, of course: no one should be prevented from enjoying that lovely part of Yorkshire and I hope the people who now live there will be resolute in protecting it against urban development, the planting of exotic trees and the overcropping of peat and turf. If not I shall have to take up my spade and shovel again on a moonlit night — but no, perhaps not!

The danger lies in the natural easy going and kindly disposition of the people there. I had an early experience of that when I was walking along the moorland road between Whitby and Pickering one day. I was carrying what was them my most precious possession, a small ·22 rifle I had won at school for shooting. As I strode along whistling to myself, a policeman rode up behind me on a bicycle, dismounted, doffed his helmet to wipe his brow and took a notebook and pencil out of his pocket. 'A'st got licence for that gun, lad?' he said. In some confusion I apologised for having neglected to get one, explained that I had only recently won it at school and assured him that I would give the matter my prompt attention. He scratched his head, replaced his helmet, notebook and pencil, and said 'Well,

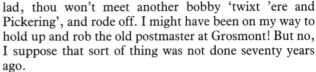

lad, thou won't meet another bobby 'twixt 'ere and Pickering', and rode off. I might have been on my way to hold up and rob the old postmaster at Grosmont! But no, I suppose that sort of thing was not done seventy years ago.

Then another man, a railway porter, was equally helpful. At the end of each term we were escorted by train to Leeds and then sent on our separate ways, each with a ticket in his hand that had been issued at Windermere. To this day I don't know what happened to mine, but it certainly wasn't in my hand or any pocket. My distress must have been obvious because a porter said to me, 'What's up, lad?' When I had explained my predicament he took five shillings out of his pocket without hesitation and handed it to me. 'Thet'll get yer to Brid,' he said. 'Oh, and 'ere's me name and address.' As soon as I got home, my father wrote to him.

About Money

Since the vulgar matter of money has been raised about my railway fare from Leeds, it is a suitable time to consider the amount Father paid per annum for me in school fees. These, in addition to board and tuition, included my carpentry classes, photographic facilities, shooting on the rifle range and swimming lessons at Kendal. The total all-in cost per boy was £100 a year. This may seem incredible at first but, as the purchasing power of the pound was then thirty times what it is now, that £100 was the equivalent of £3,000 today.

The effect of this was remarkable on our own personal finances too. Our permissible expenditure at the tuck shop, a little sweet shop in the village, was sixpence a week. Our orders were sent up on individual slips of paper to the little old lady who ran it. They were generally of this order:

Toffee buttons	1d.
Liquorice allsorts	½d.
Clear gums	½d.
Bulls' eyes	1d.
Boiled sweets (mixed)	½d.
Windermere rock	2d.
Acid drops	½d.
Total	6d. [2½p]

By a stretch of imagination, please visualise the old lady weighing out these quantities meticulously and putting them in separate little bags for each of some forty boys. I think the amount we could spend was halved later in the war. That made her task even more difficult because some of the sweets were then ordered in farthingsworth!

During the Christmas and Easter holidays my brother and I used to bicycle a lot and beagle occasionally but golf was our favourite game. As our shots were pretty wild, we had difficulty in financing an adequate supply of balls. This problem, however, we overcame. In front of the green on the first hole at Bridlington there was a large pond into which many players fluffed their approach shots. One moonlight night we went there, paddled into the water, located ball after ball in the mud with our toes, and then scooped them out with a shrimping net. These kept us going for many months.

Murder? A near miss

Some time in each year I was invited to go and stay with an uncle and aunt (she was my father's sister) who lived at Walkington, a few miles from Beverley, where they had a lovely house and three farms. My uncle had a manager or tenant on each of them but he used to visit them regularly to talk about the work and the crop prospects. His two sons who were then, I think, in their early twenties, seemed to spend all their time hunting or shooting or else at Beverley races. My aunt supervised the beautiful garden, arranged tennis parties and laid on the best breakfasts I have ever seen: the sideboard simply groaned under the load of the various hot and cold dishes. The only disadvantage there was that, as gas was not then laid on outside the towns, each one of us had to collect his or her candle from a row of them — left ready by the maid — when we went upstairs at bedtime.

When the war started my two cousins joined the army. It seems odd now but, in the Royal Artillery, they were each allowed to take one of their hunters with them to

Walkington — early twentieth century.

(*Humberside Leisure Services*)

France. They told me afterwards how they used to hunt hares and, as there were no hounds, they fired their pistols at them. My uncle scarcely ever went beyond the limits of the garden without a gun under his arm and a dog at his heels. His indoor hobby for rainy days was filling his own cartridges after they had been fired once. He and I would sit at a table with rows of empty cases, a tin of the new smokeless gun powder, packets of shot ranging from 'dust' to BB, and caps and two kinds of wads. Then there were some little measuring cups and rods to ram the wads down, a clamp to press the new caps into place and, finally, a little hand machine to turn the ends of the cases over and so seal them. The work was complicated by his having several different guns, 12 and 20 bore and a .410. It was, perhaps, tedious after a time but it was part of the game to him and I was glad to be able to help him.

He lent me the small double barrel .410 gun and taught me to use it. I became fairly good at rabbits and even had a partridge or two to my credit, but one day, unfortunately, I shot him. We had been watching a reaper binder cut a field of wheat until there remained a small island in the middle in which we knew there were some rabbits. When they began to break cover, I took the first one — but I swung my gun too far. Luckily his leggings stopped the pellets and took the blast, but each morning after that I had to recite to him the old adage:

'Never never let a gun pointed be at
  anyone,
For all the pheasants ever bred will
  not repay for one man dead.'

The End of an Era

When I returned to Windermere after that holiday, I was less homesick and unhappy than I had been before. I was glad to see my friends and was looking forward to the football. Had I a chance of getting into the 1st XI? I was undaunted by the thought of lessons. After getting a prize for work last term I should be able to cope with anything — and even rise to be the top of 1a. But, horror of horrors,

I found that I had been leapfrogged into Form 3. I thought it was a mistake and asked one of the masters. No, it was true, he said, and it meant that I should have to work far harder than I had ever done before. The world didn't come to an end and, by Easter 1916, I had gained a prize for 'General Work' in Form 5. It was a book called *The Crusades*.

Our nature walks continued but I gave up raising caterpillars. One of my most vivid memories is of the beauty of the wild daffodils in the woods near the lake. The little white pony continued to pull the mowing machine which cut the grass on the playing fields and the greedy went on cooking their disgusting meals in the Monitors' Lodge. I did manage to scrape into the football team and I still remember the excitement I felt when we went to play against Sedbergh. (The prep school, not the big one.) With cheers from the boys who saw us off at Windermere ringing in our ears, we trotted off in a horse-drawn wagonette. The sun was shining and the country was at its best but, as far as I remember, we were not. We were beaten but not disgraced and they gave us a very good tea before we started our journey back.

At the sports that year I had been beaten into second place in the hundred yards by a boy called Crosland who lived, I remember, at Crosland Lodge, Crosland Drive, Huddersfield. I expect his name — and possibly his address — will be engraved on my heart when I die, as was Calais on that of Queen Mary, because he did the same thing the next year! Two little silver cups marked '100 yards. Second prize' stand on my mantelshelf today, seventy years after my defeat. It was, however, a consolation that I won the Irving Cup for the best all rounder of the year. Father was pleased but I felt this only really meant that I was a 'Jack of all trades and master of none'. My young brother did better a few years later when he won the more important cup as *Victor Ludorum*. I shall always attribute his success to the restful time he had in his pram while I helped to push it.

The Ladder of Learning

The time had come for me to move to a public school. This was to be Repton where my two cousins who had just returned safely from the war had been. (Their name was Stephenson but, as there were several Stevensons there already, they became known as Step Hensons.) The first thing to do was to get the new clothes I should need, which entailed two journeys to a tailor in Scarborough. I thought the Eton jacket and starched collars were ridiculous: the first didn't keep my bottom warm and the collar was very uncomfortable. Why couldn't I take the sensible shorts, stockings, pullover and blazer I had worn at Windermere? The tail coat I was to wear in a year or two when I had grown taller and the sharp-edged wing collar which cut into my neck seemed even sillier. The straw boater I was to wear with these abominations didn't worry me because it was like my father's. I was to find out later, however, that they didn't last long with the treatment they had at school.

The eight houses in which we lived were scattered throughout the village and each had forty to fifty boys and

times while another had been the village inn. My heart sank when I first saw mine. After the spacious rooms, gardens and grounds at Windermere, the dark passages, cramped quarters and, worst of all, the primitive 'loos' across a yard, which were just earth closets, shocked me to the core. The front door opened from the street into the housemaster's comfortable quarters while a shabby one, which should have carried a notice saying, 'Abandon hope all ye who enter here', or, perhaps, 'Put your penny in the slot', led to ours.

Inside, in addition to the dining hall, there was a smaller common room containing a few chairs (school room type), a table and some bookshelves. We were all mainly based, however, on the study system. There were eight of these small dens, each occupied by the Studyholder, who was a house prefect or a senior boy, a 'Second' who had just risen from the fagging stage but who had no authority over fags, and then two or three fags. Each person had a chair and table space, the Studyholder, of course, having one to himself near the little coal fire. These quarters were not elegant but the fags dusted and swept them and kept them clean — but not so unnecessarily clean as we were ourselves. At times we were obliged to have three baths a day. Each morning when the bell rang to wake us up, we stripped, seized a towel, dashed down a passage and a flight of stairs and plunged into a cold bath. After games we small fry sat lined up on benches in the changing room, shivering, while the prefects and other important personages soaked for as long as they wished in the steaming hot water in the only two baths. When our turn came it was just a quick dip and out. The third bath came

Repton.

a housemaster. Most of the buildings were old neglected dwelling houses taken over for a purpose for which they were quite unsuitable. One had been a priory in ancient

on a day when it happened that the matron had put one's name down on her weekly list — and she excused no one from taking this, whatever the reason.

After several baths and a busy day one hoped for peace and quiet in the bedroom in spite of there being six boys in each. But no, that was not to be when the Head of the House chose to take his daily exercise. Simulating a run on the track with knees and feet stamping on the floor, he created a noise like a pneumatic drill. We, of course, could offer no objection. Later we had reason to regret our silent protests when he won the hundred yards at the Olympic Games. He was Harold Abrahams who has achieved added fame through the film *Chariots of Fire*.

It was not a happy time. Not only did I dislike the uncomfortable clothes we wore, the horrible little studies, the lavatories and the fagging but I missed my friends and the general friendliness at Windermere. I disliked, too, the prospect of being drilled up and down one of the playgrounds in the O.T.C. so I persuaded Sergeant Burton to take me into the band as a drummer. Another ruse of mine was to volunteer to pump the organ in chapel. This enabled me to read a book during the boring and non-singing parts of the service. I was a rebel. One thing I did notice from my point of vantage in the organ loft was that, whenever the Headmaster, Geoffrey Fisher, later to become the Archbishop of Canterbury, was preaching the sermon, everyone listened. There was none of the usual shuffling of feet and looking at watches.

In those days the way of life at school differed little from what it had been in the time of *Tom Brown's Schooldays*. Discipline was maintained and a proper respect for one's elders and betters instilled into one by fagging and, when necessary, corporal punishment. Every new boy was automatically a fag and remained one normally for a year or two, this depending on his efficiency. He was at the beck and call of his studyholder or any one of the prefects who, if no fag was in sight, would shout, 'Fag' at the top of his voice. Every fag within hearing distance had then to rush to him and the last to arrive was given the job. This could be to clean or find something, run a message to another house, bring a bun or a bar of chocolate from the school shop (the 'Grubber') or scramble him some eggs — and heaven help the fag if the toast was burnt! Almost the only job fags did not have to do was clean shoes. This was done by a little old man in a huge apron who dealt with them every evening after we had changed into slippers. He must have polished more than 6,000 shoes each term. How he must have looked forward to the holidays!

Caning was carried out not only by the Headmaster and Housemasters but by house prefects as well. There were bound to be occasional instances of prefects abusing this delegated responsibility at the first taste of power, and corporal punishment was restricted to masters only almost two decades ago. Since then the practice has virtually ceased and has been replaced by more enlightened penalties. To give a miscreant some verses of poetry to learn by heart is a more effective and beneficial punishment than caning — better both for one's brain and bottom. To this day I recall having to memorize a part of Gray's *Elegy* for some misdemeanour at Windermere and I still enjoy those verses of his. When sleep eludes one at night it can be induced by pondering over his word picture. Think of the bell tolling the curfew from the village church signalling the end of a working day. Then visualise the cows moving slowly back to their stalls — and count them as they pass. (Certainly they were lowing and could have been hungry, but that could be put right next day by moving them to another paddock or increasing their ration of silage.) The ploughman was, of course, weary but he would soon be sitting by a fire with a pint mug in his hand, 'leaving the world to darkness and to me' while 'all the air in solemn stillness holds'. If this has not had the right effect, repeat the dose — more slowly.

I was only caned, or 'swished' as we called it, once as far as I remember — and it was not a thing one easily forgot. It was for shooting a pheasant, a heinous offence which constituted poaching and theft. My crime was committed when I was walking along the road to Burton with a friend one Sunday afternoon. As we topped a hill, a beautiful cock pheasant hopped out of a ditch and ran through a hedge into a spinney. I crouched down, took out the catapult I had made and crawled

through the hedge in pursuit. In a matter of seconds, unseen, I had crept to within about five yards of it. I then let fly and got it. The mistake I made was in not plucking and roasting it as soon as we got back to the house. But it was such a beautiful bird and I was so pleased with myself at getting it that I showed it to several friends and the story got around. This taught me a lesson and, shortly afterwards, when a trap was laid for new boys, I avoided it carefully. Each year on Derby Day all the fags were recommended to climb to the top of a hill a few miles from Repton in order to see the race. I happened to know that it was being held more than a hundred miles away from Derby and I did not join the expedition.

Conversion

At some point in my third term I saw the light and decided it would be better to conform to the pattern set by the establishment. It would be less worrying for one thing. (I expect my end of term report had not been as good as my father and I had hoped.) As a start to this new plan I made myself the most alert fag in the house and gained a reputation as a 'chef' by making scrambled eggs as Alice, the matron at Windermere, had taught me. I don't claim to have shown brilliance in any other capacity but I was relieved of the burden of fagging after one year and became a House Prefect after two and a bit. The Head of the House was then Elvine Harris, as calm and sensible a man as they come. My experience with him proved a great help when I followed him as Head a year later.

Life then was fraught with responsibility and interest and, after I had cleared one stiff hurdle, very pleasant. Each year the O.T.C. held a drill competition in which the Head of each House had to command his own squad. Having been one of Sergeant Burton's drummers all my military life at school, my knowledge of drill was negligible. I was in a real dilemma. However, with some intensive cramming I managed to get by and, in fact, we did rather well, turning each time on the correct foot and no one dropped his musket.

Another incident I shall always remember was when I had to read the lesson in chapel for the first time. After mounting the step of the lectern with some trepidation, I started well enough. I had, of course, read it through before the service and knew the point at which I should stop. But it never came. I went on for a few more verses and then, in desperation, said, 'Here endeth the first lesson', and returned to my pew. After the service the Headmaster called me up and, with a chuckle, said 'Do you know what you did? You turned over two pages, you silly ass!. That was typical of Geoffrey Fisher, who was appointed Headmaster of Repton at the age of 28. He never missed a point and always saw the humour in any situation — if there was any. If there was not, one could be certain that his reasoning and determination would prevail in any gathering. Repton provided fertile ground for the production of distinguished prelates. William Temple was Headmaster before Geoffrey Fisher and both later became Archbishops of Canterbury. Then so did Michael Ramsey, who was in my study during my last year. He was a studious boy, one of the few who realised at an early age that there were more important things in life than just knocking a ball about. Consequently he attained one of the highest and most responsible positions in our land.

Reflections

What are the pre-requisites for a school to be rated as 'good'? Basically its customs and educational system must move with the times and be up to date. Most reputable schools do so gradually as a matter of course. Corporal punishment is a thing of the past and, though fagging is still practised at Repton, it is very different in form from that in my day. Fags no longer perform personal tasks for prefects but they are responsible for clearing up after meals and sweeping and tidying things generally. This is good training for the domestic chores which even some of the oldest of us now share with our wives. My wife, of course, agreed wholeheartedly with this when we visited Repton not long ago. But she took me to task, believing that I had exaggerated some of the more squalid conditions in which we lived there sixty-five years ago. In fact I had not overcoloured the horrible picture of those days but the transformation to the present conditions was far beyond my expectations. Several of the old houses had been replaced by new purpose built ones and the older ones renovated. But, in addition, I sensed a new feeling.

Had team work taken the place of the three compartments I had known; the fags, the prefects and the masters?

Is the headmaster the keystone to the quality of a school? Up to a point this is so. But even Geoffrey Fisher could not correct all the faults he may have observed at the stroke of a pen. A general could do this in the army. If he asked for a replacement of a brigade commander or a staff officer, he would get one at once. But schools and civil services operate differently: the 'axe' is replaced by 'early retirement' — and who am I to say that this is wrong? I believe, however, that the application of this should be used more frequently in the case of housemasters who are, I believe, the key men to quality in schools. When I was at Repton in the 1920's, the housemasters, with two possible exceptions, were too aloof and autocratic and too old for the job. Things are different now, better now — but not always, and, if I were about to send a great grandson to a public school, I should ascertain first by hook or by crook the name of a housemaster of whatever school who could inspire him to work hard for success in whatever his future career is to be and create a feeling of confidence and friendship with him.

My housemaster was a reserved, taciturn man who seldom spoke to us — except to say grace before and after meals. When I became Head of the House at what would now be considered the mature age of 17, he called me in to his study for a talk. He would never, of course, mention the problem of sex which, in any case, he probably thought was a four-letter word. But he did say, 'If you find there are any nasty things going on in the house, you must let me know.' I expect I replied, 'Yes, sir. Of course, sir.'

But I hadn't a clue what he was talking about.

However, a few weeks later when, at the end of term, I was travelling down to London by train, I had an experience from which I realised what he had meant. While lunching in the dining car, a man came over and asked me if the seat opposite was free. I should think I again replied, 'Yes, sir. Of course, sir', or something equally fatuous and, in the course of conversation, I explained that my father would be coming down from Yorkshire next day to join me. To cut a long story short, he asked me to meet him at his club in Dover Street. When I arrived there he said it was a very dull place and so we would go down to the Ritz for dinner. Afterwards we went on to a theatre where, during the interval, I was introduced to an actress of world renown and, when the show was over, he suggested that we should go to his flat in Chelsea for a nightcap. We did but, within a few minutes of arriving there, I was running like a hare down Cheyne Walk: *honoris causa*.

This incident concluded my non-academic education at about the same time as my only moderately successful academic one. It is a gratifying quirk of nature that, as one grows older, the memories foremost in our minds are of happy and amusing occurrences. Our mistakes and sadnesses have had their salutary effect on us and have then been relegated to the limbo of the past. Some of the incidents one recalls may be of little or no importance but they stay in one's mind just the same. What could be of less importance than my getting my house cap for football? But it was very exciting to me — and I remember well the little gold tassel it had.

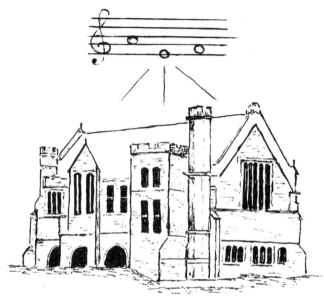

Pears School.

Anyone who lacks enthusiasm for cricket at Repton is a rank heretic fit only for burning. But now that I am an octogenarian I must confess to having been one. It seemed to me to be such a waste of time standing around in the field for hours and then batting — well, for a few minutes. Since, however, cricket has recently changed to a form of base ball, it is well worth playing and watching. But tennis, I thought, was a splendid game with its continuous action and interest. After watching and even playing a game or two with Bunny Austin who was, later, a finalist on two occasions in the Singles at Wimbledon, I became an addict to it in spite of the fact that this categorized one at Repton as a second class citizen. For sheer excitement I found nothing to equal skating. Of course none of us were very good at it in those days — and that is why it was so exciting. There were no artificial skating rinks then and our small stretch of water, Crewe's Jerry, didn't freeze every winter.

Repton would have been starved of music, which, in its various forms, provides enjoyment for more people than anything else, had it not been for the dynamic Dr. Stocks. His versatility, talent and enthusiasm merited a splendid music school such as there now is, whereas he had to teach in a few small and far from soundproof rooms next to the Boot Inn. He was no inflexible music purist: he embraced the classical and modern with equal joy, and his field of interest was wide and progressive. He composed an opera, a light one about Repton. The lyrics may not have been up to the standard of a Noel Coward or Ivor Novello but the tunes were catching and Pears School shook to its foundations when the whole school sang:

'Reptuctoo, Reptuctoo, substitute for Repton,
Now washed out and wept on,
Rep — tuc — Too!'

There is one question about him which, I fear, will never be answered. At the end of the service in chapel one Sunday morning, the voluntary he played on the organ was the theme song from *Chu Chin Chow*, which was the most popular musical show on the London stage at that time. I have often wondered whether Geoffrey Fisher had him on the mat for this — as he did me for turning over two pages.

Never having been a keen member of the O.T.C., I was not looking forward to the camp at the end of the summer term. This was nothing like an enjoyable, happy-go-lucky Boy Scout camp at which one went for interesting treks, wore comfortable clothes, cooked food over the camp fires and then had sing-songs in the evening. It was a continual struggle to be in the right place at the right time — and in the right dress. Why would one's puttees obstinately end up in the wrong place and who wanted to spend any spare time one had on polishing brass buttons, badges and boots and cleaning a rifle? It was far from comfortable, too, sleeping on the ground on straw mattresses, eight of us to an old bell tent, which was far from rainproof, and having to rush to a parade at dawn — or so it seemed — when someone blew a bugle. So, in my last year at Repton, when I was asked whether I would like to go to the Duke of York's camp instead of the O.T.C. one, I jumped at the offer.

The object of this venture was to show boys from schools like ours and others from factories and less privileged homes that they could get on well together. Some two hundred boys from widely varying environments and circumstances were to live and play cheek by jowl as equals in every way in a camp on the south coast. There would be no parades but lots of games and sea bathing. It sounded too good to be true but I said, 'Yes, please.' We had a thrilling start by being invited to lunch at Buckingham Palace. No, not in one of the banqueting rooms but in the Royal Mews. Someone said he was sure there would be turtle soup, Scotch salmon and grouse on the menu but, although there was not, we had a jolly good tuck-in before being taken down to the camp near Dymchurch in Sussex. Instead of overcrowded damp tents there were rows of neat wooden bungalows in which everyone had a camp bed. There was a larger building where the Camp Commandant gave us a welcoming talk and in which we had our meals.

We were all mixed up together, of course. It was difficult at first to get the boys from the factories to talk: they thought we were different, superior and, probably, snooty. But after we had given them a lurid and shamefully false description of life at our schools — the mass canings and the drudgery of fagging which amounted to slavery, etc., etc. — their attitude changed and they became rather sorry for us. Their lives were obviously much happier than ours.

The games were original ones. There was no cricket, rugger or soccer because they were played at our schools and we should have been at an advantage. Instead we played a sort of baseball cum rounders and a wild mass game with a soccer ball which one could kick, carry or throw. Then, of course, we bathed in the sea every day. There was only one ugly incident. On the Saturday night I and a few friends had an orgy in Dymchurch. We cannot have had more than three pints apiece at the local pub but, at that time, we were not seasoned beer drinkers and one of the party passed out. However, we managed to borrow a greengrocer's barrow and trundled him back to camp on that.

The Duke, who was later to become our King George VI, came down to spend a day and a night with us. This friendly man seemed immediately to be one of us. Dressed as were we in shorts and a shirt, he chatted with us while puffing his pipe and he then went with us for a swim. He obviously enjoyed a relaxed simple way of life. Some years later, a friend of mine got to know him well when they were in the R.A.F. together. Thereafter, once a year, he and his wife were invited to dine with the King and Queen — not in the Mews! On one of these evenings the King got up after dinner, fetched a box of cigars and offered one to my friend. To his wife's — but not his — embarrassment, he replied, 'No thank you, sir. I only smoke cigars on special occasions.'

Many years later when I was accompanying Queen Elizabeth, the 'Queen Mum', on a picnic expedition in the Aberdare Mountains in Kenya, she chuckled when I reminded her of this incident. We were sitting beside a crystal clear stream which was winding its way between rocky hills on its way from the forest, later to plunge down into the Rift Valley below us. The wild and beautiful scene was reminiscent of her native Scotland and it enchanted

her. She enjoyed the simple things of life — as well as everything else. The only difference was that we were up at 10,000 feet above sea level and, instead of herds of deer, there were buffalo and elephant. These local inhabitants were inclined, at times, to resent the intrusion into their domain by visitors— however eminent. And, as it was just about the time for their evening stroll, we decided that we should be on our way.

Thinking afterwards about this lovely day brought me up with a jerk. I had set out to write some memories of my childhood — my first. Now I am nearly in my second. I must stop.

APPENDIX

Edmund Crosskill's Journal:
Go West, Young Man

William sent his son, Edmund, to America in April 1853. This was, primarily, to show some of the implements and machinery made in Beverley at an exhibition in New York with a view to increasing exports to the U.S.A. and also for him to see as much as possible of the New World and how it was developing. Would he and his implements be welcome? The war which gained them independence from Britain had still not been forgotten by many Americans. In the event, however, it seems that Edmund was regarded as an oddity rather than an enemy — and his feelings about the Americans were much the same.

A voyage across the Atlantic in one of the paddle steamers of that time usually took about two weeks and, as they were very small in comparison with the liners of today the going was often far from smooth. Nevertheless Edmund enjoyed it. They even had a dance on deck one evening and there 'was a most agreeable lot of passengers aboard'.

On arrival at New York he stayed at the St. Nicholas Hotel: 'This is the newest hotel in New York and is most magnificently fitted up: every room is decorated in the most costly and splendid style — Although every room is so splendidly decorated there is the true emblem of a Yankee in them all and — on the landings — a spittoon which is made to accord with the style of the room fittings. It was perfectly disgusting to see the way the Americans ignored these and spat on the fine carpets.'

The exhibition was to be opened by President Pierce on the 14 July, Independence Day, so Edmund had three months in which to tour the country. But first he explored the city where neither the streets nor the girls came up to his expectations. He was disappointed to find that Broadway was not so impressive and the ladies not so well dressed as he expected: 'They wear the most expensive of clothes, have immense displays of jewellery, but want that taste to set them off which is so requisite to a *lady*. I have come to the conclusion that they are far inferior to "The Merry Maids of England".'

He planned an ambitious tour to start southward through Virginia by sea and rail. Commenting on the towns there he found that Philadelphia was 'a rapidly increasing town with good shops and tree lined streets'. He was less enthusiastic about Baltimore, merely noting that the railway carriages were warmed by stoves and

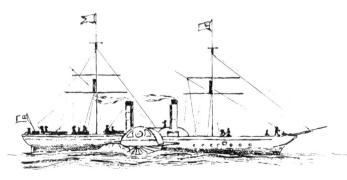

equipped with spittoons. But he had nothing but praise for Washington: 'This beautiful city' he wrote, 'has the finest streets I have ever seen, Pennsylvania Avenue being superior even to Sackville Street in Dublin.'

From Washington he went, oddly enough, by sea and rail to Richmond where he attended a slave auction: 'It certainly was horrible to see the cool manner in which the slave dealers examined the various slaves about to be sold. The first we saw sold was described as a Number 1 man without a fault. After considerable competition he was knocked down to a Jew for 1,110 dollars. The trade seemed slow for women that morning as nearly all were bought in. The slaves did not care much about being sold; some were quite unconcerned and laughed over it.'

His next move was westward by rail through the wild and beautiful Allegheny Mountains to meet the Ohio River down which he travelled on a steamer. This was not very enjoyable because, although the accommodation and the food were good, most of the passengers were pretty tough customers who rushed into the saloon at meal times where some even took the meat away in their hands. (The only point of interest to Edmund was that the average boiler pressure was only 160 lbs. per square inch!). It took eight days to reach the mouth of the Ohio and a further

five up the Mississippi and Illinois to La Salle where he transferred to a train for Chicago. This short trip was marred by part of the train running off the rails with the consequent delay of getting it back. Worse was to come but before that he was able to see and like Chicago which he described as 'a lovely place'. (Would that be mainly because he had visited a flour mill and the 'McCormack Reaping Machine Manufactory'? Or was he inspired by his first view of Lake Michigan?)

He then took a train again to cross some 200 miles of prairie to Detroit. They were soon halted, however, where a goods train had been blown off the rails and a new track was being laid. However, apart from periodical stops to drive cattle off the line, there was no further trouble and all arrived safely at Detroit which he described as 'a very nice clean improving little town'.

The next part of his journey was by steamer on Lake Erie to Buffalo. This, he said, was enjoyable, but he was only really happy when he crossed over into Canada and stayed at the Clifton House in Niagara. He found the Canadians 'far more agreeable looking and much more English-like than the people on the American side of the river'. He was obviously infected with the chauvinism of the time. Up to the point where he entered Canadian territory he had met few if any Americans he liked — or who liked him. This attitude was to change.

He was enthralled by the Niagara Falls and the rapids and spent two days studying them from both shores. He then hired a carriage and set out to visit an acquaintance, the Rector of Grimsby, a small town on the southern side of Lake Ontario. It was a precarious journey. At times the carriage was up to its axles in mud and being dragged along like a sledge. Next day his journey to Hamilton was little better by the stage which was just an open wagon: 'The road was shocking and it was a very dark night and rained in torrents the whole day. We were as nearly as possible upset as the driver could not see to avoid the holes and tree stumps with which the "road" abounded.' From there he took a steamer on Lake Ontario to Kingston. During a brief stop at Toronto he was delighted to see English soldiers on parade and all the British ships flying the Union Jack on the Queen's birthday. He then steamed down the St. Lawrence River to Montreal. This part of the journey must have been hair raising in places. He records: 'There were many rapids in the river down some of which we went at the rate of 20 to 30 miles an hour. These were considered rather dangerous and required very good steering.'

After a short visit to Quebec he returned to New York by train and enjoyed the comfort of the Metropolitan Hotel. The only thing he records about the city on this occasion was the notice posted in the New York Exchange: 'Gentlemen using tobacco are informed that no extra charge will be made for the use of the spittoons.' A week there was enough for him and, after spending a few days at a splendidly situated hotel in the Catskill Mountains, he returned to Buffalo to board a steamer bound for Lake Michigan.

The weather was bad; cold, foggy and raining most of the time. However, he had some congenial companions, three officers in the American artillery. 'We,' he wrote, 'were the only gentlemen on board and got on very well.

together.' (Was snobbery taking the place of chauvinism?) At one port of call, Mackinaw Island, Edmund went for a walk in the woods, lost his way but was guided back by some Indians. Luckily for him he arrived at the port in time for the night voyage to Sault *en route* for Lake Superior.

At that time there was no navigable waterway between Lakes Huron and Superior. Ships could steam up the St. Mary's River, the boundary between Canada and the

The journey to the hotel in the Catskills.

United States, as far as Sault but, after that, the river became a torrent rushing down a rocky gully from the higher level of Lake Superior. Ships from the upper lake had to be transported overland until a canal was completed some years later. Edmund was fascinated by the skill with which the Indians guided their bark canoes through these rapids so he did the trip with one of them. 'I had to squat in the bottom of the canoe,' he said. 'It is surprising with what dexterity they keep them from the rocks. I thought we should have been smashed to pieces many times but, just before we got to a rock, the Indian would stick his pole into the water and we just passed it by an inch. It is a most exciting sail.'

He had some good trout fishing there but shortly left for Eagle River on the south shore of Lake Superior. The weather was abominable and they were tormented by mosquitoes and 'blackflies'. Gale strength wind forced the captain to put into a small port so Edmund and four companions set off on foot to walk the twenty miles to Eagle Harbour. It was tough going and took them about seven hours. Next day, after visiting the copper mines, they started the journey back to Sault. He then crossed into Canada and boarded the S/S Kaloolah for the long sail down the eastern coast of Lake Huron where there are reputed to be 30,000 islands and, thereafter, overland to Toronto on his way to New York. It was then almost time to start his main task at the exhibition.

He reached the city a few days before the anniversary of the Declaration of Independence, 14 July. This must have been quite a day. Anyone who had a pistol or gun of any kind fired it off and squibs and crackers flew in all directions. The average number of people accidentally killed on this day each year was about forty. He spent the next four and a half months mainly at the exhibition. A large bronze medal engraved, 'Exhibition of the Ministry of All Nations, New York, 1853', is the witness of some achievement. The heat, however, was almost unbearable: during one week in August at least 200 people died of heatstroke. Nevertheless his appetite for travel and investigation seemed insatiable. With a bare four weeks left before he was due to return to England, he rushed over to Elizabethport in New Jersey to see a 'spoke manufactory', spent a day at the Latting Observatory and found time to attend a meeting of 'The Strong Minded Women Speakers' on the subject of Women's Rights. Disappointingly he did not comment on the speeches.

He then deserted the exhibition for two weeks to visit New England. He took Newport, Providence and Boston in his stride and, as usual, commented first on his hotel: 'The Albion at Boston,' he said, 'was the most comfortable I have yet seen in the United States.' After seeing a waterpowered cotton mill he went on to Portland and Gorham intent on climbing Mount Washington. As bad weather made this impossible, on he went *via* Jackson City on the White Mountain Notch to Franconia and thence to Springfield in order to see the State Armory. He was very impressed by 'some beautiful machinery for making the stocks of the muskets'. After his return to New York he visited Williamsburg to see the steampacket being built which was bound under heavy penalty to cross the Atlantic in six and a half days. As some light relief he went one day to Long Island to see a trotting match: 'There was an immense deal of gambling going on on the Race Course and the Thimbleriggers seemed to be reaping a fine harvest.'

With one week more before his departure he set out to enjoy himself: 'November 23rd Had a small dinner party. It was good fun! ... November 24th Thanksgiving Day. A party to breakfast with me — great fun all day — dancing in the evening.'

This must have been a rollicking party and one feels that his brief description of it might have been more interesting had his journal not been written primarily for his very Victorian father and mother.

On 30 November he boarded the S/S Arabia bound for Liverpool. The only excitement on this journey was seeing an iceberg some six miles away on the morning of 6 December. Cape Clear, the southernmost tip of Ireland, was seen on the 10th and they rounded the Rock Battery to reach Liverpool on the 11th. The guns fired a salute signifying the end of their voyage across the Atlantic which had taken 10 days and 18 hours.

There was a warm welcome for him when he 'returned home to Beverley by train, which I was glad to see again after an absence of rather more than eight months in which time I had been over 15,000 miles.'